Business Culture Review

By Dianne Greyson

A collection of articles about organisational behaviours and my desire to seek change, put together in this easy-to-read book

Edited by Susan Baker, BA(Hons), PGDip, MSc

Cover design by Flo Awolaja

Copyright © 2018 Dianne Greyson

ISBN: 978-0-244-13732-8

All rights reserved, including the right to reproduce this book, or portions thereof in any form. No part of this text may be reproduced, transmitted, downloaded, decompiled, reverse engineered, or stored, in any form or introduced into any information storage and retrieval system, in any form or by any means, whether electronic or mechanical without the express written permission of the author.

PublishNation
www.publishnation.co.uk

Acknowledgements

I would like to firstly thank my mother for believing in me. She has always been the driving force urging me on. I would also like to thank my husband for supporting me through the transition from employee to entrepreneur. It hasn't been an easy road but I have persevered because of the encouragement of my family.

Susan Baker, my best friend, for always being the critical ear when I wanted to do something that I thought I could not do. She has always believed in me. Jacqueline Hinds for being a friend and business collaborator who has always sought to elevate me. Lots of wise words and inspiration are given; a truly genuine individual. Dr Sylvana Storey, a powerhouse who has given insight and support. Without her foresight I may have still struggled to put this book together. I would also like to acknowledge Dr Shola Mos-Shogbamimu for stepping into the breach enabling me to move forward with the book.

To those of you reading this book, thank you for taking the time to purchase my book. I hope that you are inspired by my writing. I would also like to thank those of you that supported the #EthnicityPayGap movement by buying the T-shirt and sharing your thoughts about the articles I wrote on the subject.

A special mention to TMG and JXLSG: you are the light of my world.

Foreword

"In an era where organisational behaviour has come under increased scrutiny and heightened regulatory risk, the evolving relationship between societal values and institutional behaviour is becoming blurred. This book ushers in a refreshing insight on the power of social capital in the context of organisational behaviour. It strongly articulates the point that behavioural change comes from both the individual and organisation. To be truly progressive, we must shape organisations into a legacy that transcends the lines of division in society as well as embrace an intersectional integration that creates value and prospers on the commercial benefits of real diversity. Diversity must be at the heart of every commercial strategy and leadership.

The thought leadership shared in this book is action focused and solution oriented. It departs from the tick-box exercise approach and in exchange, the reader is taken through a factual navigation of organisational behaviour and how to address the hurdles."

Dr Shola Mos-Shogbamimu
Lawyer, Women's Rights Activist, and Founder of *Women in Leadership* publication

Contents

1. Organisational Context

2. People Management

3. Leadership

4. Employment Law (1)

5. Employment Law (2)

6. Equality and Diversity

7. #EthnicityPayGap

8. #EthnicityPayGap… Where Are We Now?

9. D&I and Emotional Intelligence: Are They on Your Agenda?

10. "Race"—The Week That Spoke Its Name

11. (Dis)Ability: Untapped Talent

12. Dyslexia: A Silent Voice in an Organisation

13. Bias or Unconscious Bias, That Is the Question

14. Psychometric Test vs Competency

15. Applicant Tracking Systems: Are They Making Us Lazy?

16. Recruitment/Talent Acquisition

17. Talent

18. Redundancy: A Slippery Slope to Poor People Management

19. Accountability

Bibliography

In Loving Memory of Stephen

Organisational Context

I have worked in different types of organisations: complex, dynamic, and agile. What they all have in common is the need for success. Success is measured in different ways which are determined by the sector they operate in, be that private, public, or voluntary (third sector).

Private organisations measure their success by market share and/or financial value. The public sector measures success by service and financial prudence. The third sector has the same measurements but must also have the ability to maintain a continuous flow of voluntary staff and funding.

Organisations play a significant part in societal growth and development so it is important that organisational behaviour reflects the positive values that make up the wider community. If this is true, why are we still hearing stories of organisations restricting the development and growth of those with protected characteristics as laid out in the Equality Act 2010? Why are some organisations not being held accountable for wrongdoing and poor performance that causes a traumatic effect on the wider community as was the case in 2008 when the banking industry unravelled?

It has been suggested that those in a position to hold organisations to account have a vested interest in keeping the organisations afloat. Some have a financial stake in them, others feel threatened by the size of an organisation and fear repercussions. An example that highlights lack of accountability is Tesco. In March 2017 Tesco was fined £129m for committing accounting fraud. One would have thought that someone would have been held to account as it is painfully obvious that the financial trail would lead to the perpetrators. On the 5th December 2018 two Tesco Directors were cleared of fraud and false accounting. Some would argue that because Tesco is such a large organisation no one will be held to account.

There is also the Barclays Libor scandal. It has been reported that the executives of Barclays were equally complicit as those that were held to account. Why were these individuals allowed to get away with not being held accountable? And finally there is G4S. It seems no matter how badly they perform they win government contracts. Why is that? Is there a secret relationship that we do not know about? The mind boggles.

The Public Disclosure Act 1998 exists to protect whistleblowers who disclose dangerous or poor practice. Unfortunately there is a stigma attached to 'whistle-blowing' as well as a fear of being sacked that makes it difficult for some people to speak out about injustices.

There have been cases where people have managed to speak out about unsound business practices such as at Sports Direct and Uber. Both have raised awareness about unfair practices.

As we now have two feet fully in 2018 we need to ask ourselves what are we prepared to accept as individuals when it comes to organisational behaviour? Will we challenge those who blatantly ignore employees within the organisation who have no voice and are being discriminated against? Will we champion positive change and help those organisations who have the intention to make the right choices, or will we forever go backwards and say there is a lack of fairness when it comes to those with protective characteristics and do nothing? It is time to say doing nothing is not an option.

We all share in the responsibility of holding organisations to account and it is important that we do so to ensure that those organisations who have lost their way or are blatantly trying to act unlawfully or unfairly are held to account. Action needs to take place and vocal champions are needed to push the initiative forward.

The rallying cry for International Women's Day was an apt one: 'Be Bold'. We need to think about the legacy we leave for those following in our footsteps. If we continually perpetuate silence and complacency there will be no progress. I would hate to think that years from now articles are still being written about the gender pay gap, lack of BAMEs at board level, LGBTQI not feeling comfortable being open about their sexuality at work, those with disabilities still having challenges getting a place at the employment table. To succeed we must challenge every aspect of negative behaviour both individual and organisational. It is time to stand up and be counted so that change can happen.

I have taken steps to make a difference by writing articles, supporting organisations not only looking to implement change but embed them. I am not the only voice; many more strong individuals are fighting to promote positive action. If we have frank discussions with organisations we can then begin to help them understand what is needed to make effective change and to allow creativity and opportunity to be more commonplace in all organisations.

People Management

Knowing the Demographics of Your Employees

It is quite interesting to know that some organisations do not give demographics any consideration. Lawrence (1997:2) points out that despite the importance, sometimes the critical role of demography, researchers often leave demographic variables "loosely specified and unmeasured, creating a 'black box' filled with vague, untested theories".

It is important that organisations are aware of the demographics of their employees to improve engagement, equality, diversity, and well-being. Demographic analysis is also important to show compliance with equal pay reporting. Gender pay gap reporting legislation will require large employers to publish their gender pay gaps from 2018. The information will include the mean and median pay. There are organisations which are not prepared for this requirement and quietly hope it will all just go away.

One could argue that an organisation could greatly improve their success rate by greater understanding of their employees. Knowing what drives them, tailoring initiatives to better target their employees' needs, advertise positions so they appeal to everyone rather than having a narrow demographic.

Success also requires you to know who is within your organisation. Some employees may wish to retire taking their knowledge with them. Are organisations prepared for this? Have they created a knowledge bank based on information gathered by their more experienced staff? If an organisation keeps 'line of sight' on the demographics of its people succession planning can be woven into their business strategy. A skills assessment can also be reviewed to ensure an agile approach to change and inform training needs.

Caring Organisation

As a consultant I have worked for many organisations. Many of those organisations have created an 'employee voice' process. This is an online process for employees to voice their opinion on the organisation. Employees have voiced that they do not bother to tell the truth or to even complete the online questionnaire because they don't believe the organisation cares anyway. Lack of engagement is generally one of the reasons employees feel unhappy.

A caring organisation in my opinion is people centred and values the contribution of its employees. It invests in initiatives to help to support and develop its employees. It has processes aligned to its values and ensures that employees are rewarded for their contribution to the success of the organisation. John Lewis Partnership would be what I would call a caring organisation.

John Lewis Partnership run an employee ownership scheme which means the organisation is wholly owned by the people who work for them. In their constitution they state, "the ultimate purpose for the business was to balance the happiness of all its members, through their worthwhile and satisfying employment in a successful business". The partnership is owned in trust for its members; they share the responsibilities of ownership as well as its rewards—"profit, knowledge and power".

Having such an approach such as John Lewis Partnership breeds inclusivity and strong values which enhances empowerment and growth within an organisation. It also cultivates development without barriers. If I were to make a criticism of John Lewis Partnership it would be that they need to work on having a more diverse board of directors.

Employee Resource Groups

It has been well documented that employee resource groups are a positive way to improve employee engagement and increase profitability of an organisation. There are many organisations that have adopted the idea of employee resource groups such as the NHS, Royal Bank of Scotland, British Telecom, TFL, and many others. The networks foster well-being and understanding through group discussion. Employee resource groups also allow organisations to have a better understanding of their employees.

There seems to be an upward trend around employee resource groups which has been put down to the willingness of organisations to improve their diversity and equality agenda. It is believed that organisations such as the ones mentioned are striving to improve the employee engagement at work and champion staff development among those who feel they have been left behind.

Action Focused

I have written many times about the lack of action some organisations take when it comes to implementing strategies to ensure the rights of their employees. I reviewed articles of organisations commenting about how they plan to change their practices to ensure they are inclusive and supportive but in reality the results do not tend to match up to their statements.

2018 should be about being action focused. We can no longer let organisations say they are going to make change without holding them to account. An 'action focused' organisation will take account of their obligation to their employees by ensuring that they support all those within it. The organisation will drive success by ensuring their employees support the vision and focus of the organisation which will in turn be supported by the policies and processes which will encourage staff to take positive action.

An organisation that has its focus on people as well as its profits will realise the greatest success. The external view of the organisation will be enhanced and its attraction levels increased.

It is no longer sufficient to be driven just by financial gain; more emphasis should be given to the people in the organisation. This approach will have a positive effect on the community at large as the experiences at work can sometimes dictate the behaviour of those working within it. I cannot state enough how important people champions are at all levels to ensure that the 'action focused' organisation embeds the ethos completely.

Leadership

There are a plethora of books written about leadership, ones that give advice on effective leadership, others that discuss the methodology of leadership, and those that try very hard to convince you that their way is the right way. I have worked for many organisations in my time and I can definitely say that the leader of each organisation has been different. My first real encounter with a leader of an organisation was within a consultancy environment. The leader wanted to be friends with everyone and delegated his responsibilities to those he trusted. He was never confrontational but I felt he never stood up to injustices within the organisation and was sometimes the perpetrator of injustices and laughed them off.

Another significant leader I worked for was a tyrant. They never had a problem giving orders and ruled with an iron fist. My memory was that of an organisation that was in fear of its leader and pushed itself into oblivion. I felt it was my responsibility to be supportive as best as I could in that situation by listening and advising those who needed help.

In my career journey I have myself been in leadership positions running divisions of large organisations. What was always important to me was ensuring my staff felt supported and that I was delivering on organisational objectives. There is a term for that now: Emotional Intelligence (EI). Although for me having emotional intelligence is a natural state of mind I have now come to realise that not everyone has this ability.

Jacqueline A. Hinds, Chair of the Society of Emotional Intelligence UK Chapter, believes that organisations need to improve the knowledge and understanding of emotional and cultural intelligence across all levels of their workforce; this will enable them to build upon the organisation's visions and values, empowering their workforce by embedding these practices and principles through understanding employee engagement initiatives, respecting and valuing each other from an equitable organisational platform.

Leaders play such an important part in sculpting the values of an organisation. Employees look to them to fashion behaviours within an organisation. When I hear of the lack of equality and diversity in an organisation I ask myself, "What is the leader doing to improve the situation?" It is the leader's vision that employees follow and they set out the terms of engagement for the organisation. It is all well and good to suggest that the Human Resources (HR) department drive a process to improve equality and diversity but if the leader is not championing this process then it is already dead in the water. It requires executive leaders, divisional leaders, and operational managers to champion effective strategies. If it is only HR taking the lead in promoting positive strategies they will no doubt encounter blockages along the way thus causing a delay in implementation.

So what is needed? A 'synergised' solution that allows the leader to empower others to drive efficiency within the organisation, utilising emotional intelligence, equality, diversity, and people power through employee resource groups. As the leader is the driving force of an organisation it has the power to disseminate these skills by posting champions through the business.

There is already evidence out there that shows the benefits of improving thoughtful leadership. We need to change the way we think about leadership to improve not only the results of an organisation but the well-being of its employees.

I know that the NHS is trying to make positive moves to improve its leadership teams by tapping into a talent pool that already existed but had not been cultivated. They have taken positive steps to improve the promotional prospects of BAME staff by implementing a leadership and mentoring programme. The NHS has chosen to think differently about leadership and understands that it is important to offer a more open and inclusive approach. It is too early to know if statistics will identify any improvement in engagement of employees, well-being, service delivery, and patient care but I feel confident that once the changes embed themselves the evidence will show that there will be a significant upturn.

Leadership is key to any organisation but it must be the right leadership. A thoughtful leader who can inspire, teach, guide, and support is paramount to having a successful organisation. A disruptive leader will only create negativity, low employee engagement, poor value systems, and will no doubt cause future damage to the organisation's reputation. The disruptive leader may be perceived as a financial winner but at what cost? Are leaders open enough to take criticism and make the right changes to improve the structure of their organisations?

I think it is tough being a leader as you have the responsibility of others and you are looked upon as the driving force but if you make the right choices when coming to leadership style, you can eliminate some of the stresses that come with leadership. The approach you take will determine the outcome of not only your organisation's profitability but your employees' ability to succeed and develop.

Employment Law (1) 2015

The definition of law from Google web:

    1. The system of rules which a particular country or community recognises as regulating the actions of its members and which it may enforce by the imposition of penalties. "Shooting the birds is against the law."
    2. Synonyms: rules and regulations, system of laws, body of laws, constitution, legislation, code, legal code, charter; jurisprudence, "the law of the land".
    3. A rule defining correct procedure or behaviour in a sport. "The laws of the game."
    4. Rule, regulation, principle, convention, direction, instruction, guideline, practice, "the laws of the game".

I am sure there are more detailed definitions out there but from my experience this is a very accurate one. Some organisations can't seem to understand they have a lawful duty to behave in a certain way. Why is it that we seem to be seeing a significant growth in complaints relating to organisations acting unlawfully when it comes to employment law? Is there a lack of understanding about employment law? Do organisations respect the law? There are ways and means out of violations of employment law, for example the non-disclosure agreement. Is it time for us to get rid of this tool which is often being used to hide serious breaches of legislation?

Human Resources should no longer be bullied by those within an organisation who avoid dealing with grievances in an appropriate manner. Smaller organisations without Human Resources should not be excused in their behaviour either. Employment law is there to help organisations to operate appropriately. There should be no excuse.

People make an organisation, let's not forget that. The law is there to protect employees and organisations to help to facilitate a positive working environment.

Employment Law (2) 2018

In 2015 I wrote an article about how some organisations have shown a blatant disrespect for the rule of law. The reason why I have decided to revisit the issue of employment law was because of Carrie Gracie. Carrie Gracie, BBC China Editor, gave evidence to the House of Commons Digital, Culture, Media and Sport Committee in January 2018. She spoke of her disbelief when she found out that she was being paid less than her male counterparts. She is not the only BBC female journalist or editor in this position. It now transpires that there are over 100 women that have pay disparities.

I was once put in a position when asked by a director to offer a male senior manager more than a female senior manager. I pointed out to the director under the Equality Act 2010 it was unfair to pay a female employee differently than a male employee for doing the same work. I went on to inform the director that if the female employee was to find out she would have a case against the organisation which would be duly upheld. The director said OK but still asked me to make the offer. I was aware that if I spoke to the CEO about what had just occurred he would do nothing to help as he himself embarked on some unfavourable practices.

I have come across two types of HR executives in my career; those who like me outline the importance of ensuring the organisation complies with employment legislation and others who turn a blind eye. The latter cultivate unethical and unlawful behaviour and discriminatory working environments.
Employees often have limited knowledge and understanding of employment legislation. They may feel aggrieved they do not realise they have protection under the Equality Act 2010. It

surprised me that Carrie Gracie stated that she did not know her rights relating to equal pay under the Equality Act 2010. I wonder how many more people out there are in the same position.

Employment law should have parity with criminal law. Tougher action needs to be taken when organisations and individuals act unlawfully.

During the early stage of my career I was asked to draft a non-disclosure agreement. I decided to resign from the organisation because I could not accept that they were willing to sweep things under the carpet and pay off someone who really deserved their day in court.

Being in HR has great rewards if you really want to play a part in the development of the organisation. Strong employee engagement comes from giving support, nurturing, and valuing. If organisations wish to behave like bullies their employees will become negative, unresponsive, and uncaring.

Employees, know your rights, you can go online for information and guidance. Those of us in HR have a part to play to support employees and make them feel that they will be listened to and know that action will be taken against wrongdoing.

Equality and Diversity

When I publish a post I like to make it punchy and not too long. The reason behind this lies in the fact that I have always believed that I was dyslexic. I have never been tested but I have some of the traits outlined in the spectrum. One particular trait is the anxiety caused by reading long text. I suddenly get headaches and my eyes start to hurt. To cope with this I started out gliding through text skipping huge chunks of words out but always getting the meaning. For those of you who are dyslexic, please feel free to glide through my writing and pick out the words that resonate with you.

The Equality Act 2010 was introduced to ensure that employees who have particular characteristics are protected from discrimination. Those characteristics are: age, disability, race, marriage and civil partnership, religion or belief, gender reassignment, sex, sexual orientation, pregnancy, and maternity. Since this act was implemented it was hoped that there would be a dramatic change in the way that organisations viewed those working within their organisation. More transparency, honesty, and fairness would give rise to equal treatment. Although there has been some shift, the movement towards equality in my opinion is slight. Evidence-based research shows we still have many rivers to cross.

Roger Kline, Research Fellow at Middlesex University Business School, wrote a report called 'Snowy White Peaks' addressing the issue of BAME treatment within the NHS and the lack of diversity at leadership level. This was written in March 2014. In 2016 the NHS published a Workforce Race Equality Standard (WRES) detailing the experiences of BAME and white staff. The WRES highlighted the bullying, harassment, and lack of progression experienced amongst BAME staff. This is a must-read for anyone who would like to look at the realities of BAME people in the workplace.

The Equal Opportunities Commission reported in November 2016 that almost half of 440,000 pregnant women in the UK experienced some form of disadvantage simply for being pregnant or taking maternity leave. It was also reported that 30,000 women had been forced out of their jobs. There have also been countless reports about the lack of women on boards of directors.

In 2014 *The Guardian* published an article identifying that 34% of LGBT individuals would not come out openly at work for fear of unfair treatment. Transgendered people tend to suffer more discrimination at work and feel threatened in some cases. There have been notable cases such as the 'gay cake' row when a bakery refused to make a pro gay marriage cake.

On 3rd January 2017 *BBC News* reported on an incident when Anne Wafula Strike, a Paralympian, was unable to use the disabled toilet on a train as there was a fault with the toilet provision. I mention this particular case because it highlights the lack of adjustments organisations are making to help those with disabilities.

Without going into details I once had to insist that a senior member of an organisation interview a candidate who required reasonable adjustments. He gave me all the excuses under the sun not to see her. I however was firm and reminded him of his legal obligation. That was the end of that. She was hired in the end which was great but how many cases have not ended well?

We have a long way to go to improve the statistics above and change the headline to more positive ones which should reflect the positive changes that should be made at this time. There are organisations pursuing change through sifting through data analysis. As we know, data can be manipulated and it is a cold solution without involvement of equality and diversity champions to translate that data into action. But what is the real measure that demonstrates success? Is it how many BAME staff we have hired or promoted? Or is it the fact that we have allowed an LGBT person to feel comfortable being themselves? I suggest that neither of these could be a true indicator.

Should we reject the division/partitioning of employees with protected characteristics? I have seen job titles such as Head of People/People Director; these titles reflect an action I think should be taken. Let's start talking about people and their needs and treating employees equally when making decisions. It is not enough to create programmes for an individual group, it should be for the organisation.

Organisations will now have to reflect on their own behaviours and really hold themselves to account for the breeding of negative cultures. Tough questions will need to be asked of those at senior level. Equally tough measures will be required to be made operationally to ensure that bullying, harassment, and all types of discrimination are eradicated by embedding the right organisational values into the company and creating appropriate processes and procedures to match.

To embed equality and diversity where none exists requires organisational commitment which starts from the top and is cascaded down to the bottom. A culture of intolerance towards those who seek to damage the integrity of an organisation is required. Organisations should be driven by and concerned about ALL the people working for them and they should ensure that everyone is encouraged to stay away from recruiting 'people like them' and embrace the reality of the difference in this world.

A colleague of mine, Dr Terence Jackson, once commented, "We only have to look at nature to see that diversity is the key to life. Allowing everyone to play an equal part enhances the ability for growth".

If we do not see champions of equality and diversity in organisations at every level, change will be prevented from flourishing. Do not let gatekeepers of the negative past stop your organisation from moving forward. There is evidence that suggests that organisations will benefit financially from having a more inclusive organisation.

#EthnicityPayGap

This is the pay gap that no one seems to want to talk about. When the conversations do materialise they are quickly glossed over in favour of further discussions about the equal pay gap. The gap between men and women is indeed an important topic but surely we cannot have a resolution unless we also address the ethnicity pay gap. This gap is highest when we discuss the difference between white women and women of colour.

In America the issue around the ethnicity pay gap is already a discussion topic. *Maclean's*, a Canadian publication, highlights the issue of women of colour suffering two pay gaps, that of men and women and because of their race. The Equality and Human Rights Commission have also undertaken research about the ethnicity pay gap. In fact, if you Google search this topic you will observe that there have been quite a few undertakings on this subject.

Why are organisations not addressing this issue? I have had many discussions around the ethnicity pay gap with fellow colleagues and what seems to be a common thread is the need for action now. I recently read a thread on LinkedIn originating from Vanessa Vallely OBE who highlighted an article by Leana Coopoosamy on the gender pay gap entitled "What about Ethnicity?". It was this thread and article that made me realise that I had to step up and do more to make this subject more visible. I created the hashtag #EthnicityPayGap to be the catalyst to create a movement. The many positive comments about the #EthnicityPayGap made me realise there are people ready to protest and act. Dr Joanna Wilde, contributor to the book *Racism At Work*: "this issue is a workplace health issue". She was acknowledging the anxiety and stress that is caused knowing that you are being paid less because of your colour. Another response, this time from Roger Kline, Research Fellow at Middlesex University Business School, who clearly demonstrated the organisation context by observing that "the Ethnicity Pay Gap will highlight occupational segregation, concrete ceilings for recruitment and promotion and the impact of discretionary pay systems".

We know that the BBC has been under the spotlight regarding equal pay and I with many others have written about it. As I said earlier equal pay is important but this will never be achieved without addressing the ethnicity pay gap. Are companies willing to address this? Currently I would say not but critical voices are starting to increase in this area. Afua Hirsch, an author and writer for *The Guardian*, is one of those voices that have been putting a light on the ethnicity pay gap. She looks into the issues and uses the BBC as an example of an organisation ignoring the ethnicity pay gap.

There is a lot of statistical information out there that bears out the fact that the ethnicity pay gap does exist. As with other areas that look at the treatment of diverse groups, producing statistics really does not create a paradigm shift in attitudes. In my opinion, what makes a difference is collective voices. You cannot be ignored if you speak in one articulate voice with evidence to back you up.

What is stopping us from creating a voice to challenge the ethnicity pay gap? It's a real issue that exists and the time is now to make things happen.

When you see articles on equal pay, please comment by using #EthnicityPayGap to keep the issue out there. If you are on a panel talking about equal pay, mention #EthnicityPayGap and if your colleague mentions how important it is to get equal pay mention the #EthnicityPayGap.

#EthnicityPayGap... Where Are We Now?

In April 2018 I wrote an article about the ethnicity pay gap. I wrote the article to raise awareness about the issue. It received a great response and it made me realise more needed to be done.

Whenever possible I shared my views on the subject using the hashtag that I created, #EthnicityPayGap, and asked others to follow suit to raise the profile. As I continued talking and writing about the topic I began to realise months had passed and not much had changed. That is when I hit upon a great idea.

Although in my head I thought it was a good idea I wondered how it would be perceived. I am not one who believes in making myself the brand but I knew I had to do something. It was then I decided to design a T-shirt using the hashtag that I created to show my support in raising the issue. I took a photo of myself in the T-shirt and posted it on LinkedIn. I was not quite ready for what happened next. People commented how great it was that I put myself out there to support the cause. Not only that, they wanted a T-shirt too. At no point had I thought about making the T-shirt available for others but because of the interest I started to research suppliers to recreate the T-shirt.

The orders started coming through from the UK and America. I asked people to post pictures of themselves wearing the T-shirt; this is when the movement really gained momentum. Whilst I focused on keeping the #EthnicityPayGap movement going, I began to hear about reports that further gave weight to the movement's existence.

In July 2018, ITN reported its ethnicity pay gap. The mean pay gap was 16.1% and mean bonus was 66%. Prior to this Deloitte reported on their ethnicity pay gap. This was reported in December 2017. It showed that the ethnicity pay gap mean was 12.9% and the bonus was 41.9%. The Department of Business, Energy and Industrial Strategy (BEIS) commissioned a report which was written by Ruby McGregor-Smith; the report found that the economy would be likely to benefit significantly if BME employees were given the same opportunities as their white counterparts.

The government has commissioned new research this year into how organisations are trying to get rid of their ethnicity pay gap. With all this gathering of evidence why isn't the outcry louder? Surely the ethnicity pay gap has its roots in discrimination. It's not only because those who are not white do not get the same opportunities but some organisations deliberately decide not to pay the same salary for the same job because they felt they could get away with it, or are we not worth the same money?

A cross party meeting was held in Parliament on 23rd October 2018 to discuss ethnicity pay gap reporting. I can only hope that something constructive comes out of this. Equality in pay cannot be attained without first addressing the ethnicity pay gap. The ethnicity pay gap will not be rectified without our voices being heard.

The #EthnicityPayGap movement is one way to raise awareness. People may view it as insignificant but the more support it gets the more people will see it thus creating a talking point. If you would like to be part of the movement, my company Equilibrium Mediation Consulting have #EthnicityPayGap T-shirts for you to order.

I planned to conclude my article with the comment above but I was given a newspaper report by the *Guardian* newspaper identifying that there was a disparity of pay between black medics and white medics. I couldn't believe I was seeing this again. This article was written on 27th September 2018 and it demonstrates to me that there is a lot more work to do.

D&I and Emotional Intelligence: Are They on Your Agenda?

Diversity & Inclusion is important not just for organisations but for society. You can say much the same about Emotional Intelligence. Diversity & Inclusion and Emotional Intelligence offer a holistic approach to people management.

Currently there are many providers offering training in these areas and I believe there are exams you can take to specialise in both. It is of course a good idea to have people who can focus on these areas in an organisation, either a consultant such as myself being invited for a short period of time to support a pending strategy, or someone already within the organisation who will champion these areas to ensure that everyone becomes 'mindful'.

We can overcomplicate things. What I mean by this is, shouldn't we all have these skills in our toolkit? Some people are naturally aware of diversity and inclusion and emotional intelligence and how this really should be a day-to-day consideration. I have throughout my career been a champion of Diversity & Inclusion and Emotional Intelligence before these words had even been uttered amongst the business community.

We need more champions of Diversity & Inclusion and Emotional Intelligence not just to train and coach but to embed into practice. We need to learn from organisations such as the NHS who not only have this on their agenda for learning, they are embedding good practice. They are continuously recognised as diversity champions. It makes me wonder why companies such as Apple, Facebook, et al. have difficulty improving their diversity status, and CEOs are still cited as having limited or no Emotional Intelligence.

Many studies have already shown the positive benefits of a diverse organisation and the importance of Emotional Intelligence. Both give organisations a competitive edge and improve employee engagement.

If you have decided to embark on training/coaching in Diversity & Inclusion and Emotional Intelligence make sure you have a budget for embedding the process. The organisation must believe in the process at all levels and ensure that the management team champions 'mindfulness' with all its positive attributes.

"Race" — The Week That Spoke Its Name

I was very fortunate to be a guest of Diane Greenidge at the Investing in Ethnicity & Race Conference 2017. This was a great event that highlighted the issues that many face within organisations about race and discrimination. It seems that organisations are not keen to have informed discussions with their employees that would allow for open and honest discussions to tackle the inherent racial bias that some organisations cultivate.

One of the workshops I attended was 'BAME Inclusion— Starting a Conversation', facilitated by Melissa Berry. One particular topic touched on the perception of racism versus stereotyping. It was argued that saying that someone from a difference race or country works hard is a stereotype and making a similar statement changing the message to be a negative one ("these people are lazy") could be seen as racism.

In the final part of Melissa's session she spoke about a video which I had also seen demonstrating how white privilege worked ($100 Bill Race). A white lady in the audience raised her hand and said, "We need to be careful about saying that there is white privilege for all white people." I became quite annoyed about her statement and raised my hand to reply to her comment. I stated that "white privilege is a systemic issue in society and within organisations. The term demonstrates that being white is a benefit at all stages of life because it seems to be the colour of preference". I did not like her condescending tone either and I wondered why she was there. I came to realise it is people like her we need to have in the room to widen their understanding of being BAME in this society. Sometimes we preach to the converted rather than to those who are on the border or just outright ignorant of the changes that need to occur.

The whole day was full of great nuggets of information and lots of nodding heads when it came to reflecting on experiences being BAME employees. There was a shared understanding that something had to change and we must be the pioneers of that change. Speakers such as Dawn Butler MP, Mark Lomas, Paulette Mastin, and others gave us insight into their thoughts about the lack of BAME representation particularly at board level. A particular takeaway for me was when Dawn Butler MP suggested that there should be a central place to find 'best practice' with regard to BAME engagement, development, and progression programs in the workplace for employers to review and implement.

My week became even more eventful when I joined the Silent March for Grenfell Tower. It was great to be part of this movement. When I walked with my candle around Ladbroke Grove a thought struck me, there was a parallel to the event I attended earlier that week and the march: BAME people being ignored and their right to be heard being muffled. The pain I saw that day was palpable and it moved me greatly. Societal responses to BAME people are often mirrored in the way some organisations treat their BAME staff.

Grenfell was an awful tragedy that should not have happened; the people who survived and social commentators have regularly observed that if the demographics of those who lived in the tower were different this awful tragedy would not have happened.

We have had the Lammy Report, Race Disparity Audit, Parker Review, the McGregor-Smith Review, and others all saying the same thing. Why are we not seeing change? How many more reports/reviews do we have to have before real change happens? Organisations are still closing the door to BAME representation and getting away with it; why are they not being held to account? Equally tragedies such as Grenfell demonstrate that discrimination permeates throughout the UK infrastructure causing BAME individuals to be treated unfairly in all aspects of daily life.

We need to speak in a collective voice that will resonate with those in power and influence. Silence is not an option if you want real progress to be made. Being a disrupter is not a bad thing if what you are trying to disrupt is a negative force. Be proud that you have stood up for injustice and encourage the young to do the same.

(Dis)Ability: Untapped Talent

I often wonder why it is so hard for organisations to employ people with disabilities. The Equality Act 2010 has sufficient guidance to give organisations an informed process to follow. It is clear that it is discriminatory to treat a disabled person unfavourably because of something connected with their disability. This type of discrimination is unlawful. If the employer knows of the disability, reasonable adjustments are to be made.

Does the Equality Act 2010 go far enough to ensure that organisations comply? Some people believe the Equality Act has no teeth. Should we look at the role that HR plays in enforcing the law around employment?

Disability discrimination is against the law so why are there so few disabled people in work? I once worked for an organisation who declined an internal candidate because they had a disability. The manager said they could not the make reasonable adjustments needed to allow her to do the job. I took responsibility to remind the manager that by not interviewing this candidate he was acting unlawfully. The only adjustments the candidate would require would be to their workstation; more importantly, she had the skills required for the position. Using a knowledgeable but firm approach with the manager, I was able to ensure that the candidate had an interview, and moreover, she got the job.

The relationship between HR and organisational operations can be a challenging one. There are HR departments who are driven by operations, causing conflict between what HR believe is right and what operations say they require. Sometimes it seems that both are at odds with each other when they should be working seamlessly.

HR and operations can come unstuck even at the initial stage of employment. The selection process is meant to sift out unsuitable candidates but can also be used to avoid difficult discussions with disabled candidates. Fear can be a strong driver in these situations, not knowing how to incorporate the disability, the perceived cost of hiring a candidate with a disability, and sadly, perceived culture fit.

When I worked as a HR consultant for the Metropolitan Police Service in 2014, I was impressed with the diverse culture they had managed to cultivate in their corporate services office. I was able to witness people with disabilities working alongside their fellow colleagues making the same contribution to the organisation.

There are people making positive moves to support individuals with disabilities, four of whom I am connected with on LinkedIn: Elizabeth Kwarteng-Amaning, Julian John, Christopher Catt, Martyn Sibley, and Gary Denton. Some of these individuals work on a local level and others on a national level. Why not speak to them and find out how you can hire a person with a (dis)ability?

Dyslexia: A Silent Voice in an Organisation

I have had many successes in my career which have included some senior level appointments. To get to a senior level was not an easy task. I have now come to realise that I was hiding my dyslexia. I did not do this intentionally as I hadn't realised that I was dyslexic until I was fully established as a professional individual.

I was introduced to Elizabeth Kwarteng-Amaning, CEO of Aspire2inspire Dyslexia. The organisation supports both adults and children with dyslexia to fulfil their dreams and aspirations. I was asked by Elizabeth to be a speaker at an event for entrepreneurs with dyslexia which I duly accepted. At the time she was aware that I had not had a formal assessment and offered to make this happen.

Making the decision to accept the assessment made me ask some questions. If I was formally diagnosed as being dyslexic what will it mean for my future? Would I give companies another reason not to use my services? I am fully aware being a black woman entrepreneur has its challenges; to add dyslexia to this could give companies even more reason not to use my services. I decided to undertake the assessment regardless and I received positive confirmation that I am indeed dyslexic.

My journey has made me wonder how many other people out there have suffered in silence or just accepted that they are dyslexic so they can be treated equally? I fell into the camp that just accepted their dyslexia. I wonder, is this the same for those with mental health issues? Do people stay silent because they feel it's best to suffer in silence rather than get support from their employers or in fear of losing their jobs? A charity campaigner, Rosa Monckton, wrote a piece for *The Spectator* suggesting that it should be possible to pay people with learning disabilities less than the minimum wage to make it an incentive for employers to hire people with learning disabilities. I personally do not agree with this; it opens the floodgates to make it acceptable to pay people less because they do not mirror the person who is hiring them.

My dyslexia is a mild form but those with more severe difficulties have more visible signs that may be easier for companies to detect. It is usually the employee however that informs the employer and reasonable adjustments are made to support them. I cannot help but draw comparisons again with those with mental health challenges. Employees struggling with mental illness are not likely to be visible to employers and unlike dyslexics are less likely to inform their employer because of stigma.

The Equality Act 2010 highlights the need to prevent discrimination. Mental illness and dyslexia fall under the umbrella of 'protected characteristics' so should we feel comforted that we will not be discriminated against when applying for jobs, offering services, or seeking promotion because the Equality Act 2010 protects us? Well, it should. The importance here is you must challenge any situation that leads you to believe that you are being discriminated against because of disability, sex, or racial make-up.

The theme for International Women's Day was 'Be Bold'. Boldness takes many forms; speaking out against inequality is one, talking about your situation is another. Both are of equal importance in helping you reach your goals. Boldness is an important piece of armour in this day and age. We need to speak out when injustices are visible and seek to change the mindsets of those who do not support equality in the workplace or in society.

I hope to report that in the future that my discovery of being confirmed dyslexic has not hindered my ability to bring in business. I hope I can show that I have enhanced my opportunities. If you feel that you are being discriminated against, do something about it. Equality must be the future for business and we should fight discrimination of any kind. Fairness makes employees feel valued and appreciated. Those organisations that do not have fair practices can be guaranteed low employee engagement and lower financial returns.

Bias or Unconscious Bias, That Is The Question

The unconscious versus conscious debate annoys me. Why? Because the net result underplays the dangers and realities of conscious bias. To understand my thought process I thought it useful to identify the definition of both.

The Definition of Unconscious Bias

Professor Uta Frith, DBE, FBA, FMedSci, FRS on behalf of The Royal Society provides a useful and widely accepted definition, which is that unconscious bias occurs when we make judgments or decisions on the basis of our prior experience, our own personal deep-seated thought patterns, assumptions, or interpretations, and we are not aware that we are doing it.

The *Stanford Encyclopaedia of Philosophy* study on implicit bias first publicised in 2015 refers to "implicit bias" as relatively unconscious and relatively automatic features of prejudiced judgment and social behaviour.

The Definition of Conscious Bias

From *Psychology Today*:

"A bias is a tendency. Most biases—like the preference to eat food instead of paper clips—are helpful. But cognitive shortcuts can cause problems when we're not aware of them and apply them inappropriately, leading to rash decisions or discriminatory practices. Stereotype threat, for example, is the confirmation of negative stereotypes about another person's race, gender, group, and so on."

Oxford Dictionary:

"Inclination or prejudice for or against one person or group, especially in a way considered to be unfair."

I do not necessarily have an issue with the definition of bias as it gives a description of those who do not like things or people because of how they feel about them. It is not a matter of applying negative thoughts inappropriately; it's simply that the individual is choosing to take the stance which makes them feel better.

When it comes to talking about unconscious bias, this is where I struggle. I struggle because I do not believe bias can be unconscious; that would infer the person is asleep? Or their brain is not engaged? Yes, there are eminent people out there that have made a case for unconscious bias but in reality is this not a way to create a 'get out of jail' card for those who harbour bias towards others? One is sometimes compelled to use the phrase to keep up with buzzwords in the marketplace. I myself have done so, using it within my CV. I have however deleted all mention of unconscious bias from my CV because I feel that strongly about it.

I met with a colleague of mine, Jiten Patel, who co-wrote the book *Demystifying Diversity*. Jiten is a great equality and diversity champion and we often have discussions around this area. During our recent meeting we discussed unconscious bias and I of course gave him my opinion. He offered another perspective, that of inherent bias, a world view that exists in all of us as a permanent characteristic or attribute. This definition is more in line with my beliefs as I believe bias is inherent in the way you are brought up and what you are exposed to.

Inherent bias is a strong and definitive way that shows people where their bias may stem from. If you get people to look in the mirror they can then view the change they need to make. This is the same for organisations; inherent bias in organisations is rife and needs to be challenged by those willing to speak out. We must stop softening the reality of bias and give it the name that it needs to play a significant part in challenging organisational behaviour, employee engagement, and employee-to-employee interaction.

I am sure there are those of you out there that feel comfortable with the concept of unconscious bias and feel my view is unfounded. That's OK, you must work with what makes you comfortable, but I do feel that we who champion the benefits of a diverse workforce need to strengthen our choice of language for maximum impact. The term 'inherent bias' challenges the narrative that discriminatory behaviour is unconscious. There are too many stories circulating about poor behaviour of organisations and individuals towards people in minority/marginalised groups. I for one will not stand for this type of behaviour to continue. I will call out bias when I see it and I will defend those who need my support.

Action to combat discrimination towards people from BAME backgrounds and those with disabilities needs to be addressed now! I do not want to look at another report highlighting pay gaps or under-representation, or see another diversity conference without any diversity in the panel. Action is the only thing that will make things change and reduce the bias that is currently inherent in the workplace and the community.

Psychometric Test vs Competency

There have been many discussions about the use of psychometric assessment vs competency assessments, the main one being which one will give the best results. I don't believe there is a definitive answer to that question. I think the question should be which one works for you?

As with most situations, you need to have a strategy. The first should be to identify the positions you need to recruit for and look at the remit of the role. The seniority of the role will determine which recruitment assessment tool you should select. You should also note which attributes you wish to identify during the assessment.

I applied for a senior talent acquisition consultant position at a high-profile social media company. The first stage of their interview process was a psychometric assessment. I have done many of these assessments before but what made this one different was the irrelevance to the role. The psychometric assessment given was a mathematical one which in my mind would not identify whether I was good for the role or not. What would have been more appropriate would have been an assessment that identified my personality traits, work style, and practical experience of working in similar positions.

My positive experience of psychometric testing had been when I was given a Myers Briggs psychometric test as part of a development review. This test was a very good test for me as it was highly relevant to my role as a lead resourcing/HR business partner.

Psychometric and competency-based assessments can work effectively hand in hand, whereas competency-based assessments can be used in isolation; I do not think the same for psychometric testing.

When dealing with high volume recruitment you may wish to run an assessment centre. Again one should be clear from the outset what skills and personal attributes you are trying to assess. You can hire an external firm to provide an assessment service or you can buy one 'off the shelf' which you can tailor to your needs. Having chosen which avenue you wish to travel you should be ready to select the appropriate individuals within the organisation that can deliver the assessment. Even when using an outside company you should also ensure that you have internal employees involved.

It is possible that psychometric testing and competency-based testing can prevent bias by making a decision based on the result rather than the person. However, there are ways for the result to be manipulated, which was bought to my attention by an occupational psychologist. Assessments based on CVs can be vulnerable to bias. In some instances it can give away a person's ethnicity. There are also questionnaires given that ask participants to define their race, religion, sexuality, etc., risking poor process management.

If the assessments are managed appropriately, the tools can be used not only for general recruitment but as part of a diversity drive, to assess inherent bias and aptitude for emotional intelligence of both internal and external candidates.

Choose wisely, take the time to review your needs and identify the results you are looking for, and make sure you have the right people undertaking the process.

Applicant Tracking Systems: Are They Making Us Lazy?

Applicant tracking systems (ATS) have been around for many years. They have evolved to become significant players when it comes to resourcing for candidates.

I am not sure if anyone out there remembers Cardbox? Cardbox was a database system which allowed you to input information about candidates and write general comments about the candidate. This system allowed you to search for keywords and would at the end of the search give you a list of candidate names to choose from. Now your work did not stop there; you would then look at the candidate's application and review their skills further, and if you felt you had a match you would then call the candidate to discuss their skills in more detail and get a better idea if there was a fit with your client's specification.

ATS systems today such as I-Grasp, Taleo, TribePad, and many others are more intelligent than Cardbox. The candidate's information is collected, the candidate's application is reviewed and deselected at a push of a button. Time is saved which allows the individual to move forward with other projects.

The ATS systems are indeed clever but are they making us lazy? What has happened to the contact between the hirer using the ATS system and the candidates? I think within a recruitment agency environment it seems to have had more of an impact when it comes to the relationship with their candidates. I have come across many blog posts that bemoan the lack of communication from recruitment agencies. Could it be that there is an over-reliance on ATS systems managing the candidate process?

What about HR? Do they suffer a similar problem in that the ATS system is used to manage the candidate journey whilst they become involved in other HR issues? Even those solely focused on recruitment can become too dependent on the ATS system. I myself have fallen foul of this, particularly when I was managing sixty vacancies per week; you rely heavily on the system to process information quickly.

When using an ATS system you are involved in a formal process which can diminish your ability to be creative. What I mean by this is looking deeper into a candidate's skillset and reviewing it without allowing yourself to think it doesn't tick that box so therefore they not suitable.

There is also the risk of bias. Depending what filters are set on the ATS system, bias can be present at this stage causing candidates to be deselected before their full application has been reviewed. I remember working for one organisation who added a health questionnaire onto their ATS system and an Equality and Diversity form.

These two forms were not to be used as part of the selection process, however the organisation allowed managers access to the information held on the forms. It is my belief that managers used both forms to deselect candidates.

We should not be a slave to the ATS system; we must stop ourselves from becoming zombies and use the system to engage our minds to greater effect. We should allow more communication and support of those applying for jobs. We should remember that we have livelihoods in our hands and we must go over and above to ensure we have managed the process appropriately.

Recruitment/Talent Acquisition

When I started out, rules around recruitment were limited. No one cared very much about diversity, hours of work, advertising guidelines, etc. Organisations were free to do what they wanted without issue and staff were treated unfairly in some cases. Now organisations invest more time in recruitment and take time to assess skills more intently. Some members are trained in this area and external consultants such as myself are used to support their hiring process.

There are a plethora of systems and processes out there to assist in recruitment: ATS, psychometric testing, assessment centres, and personality testing such as Myers Briggs. With all of these things and more at our fingertips, why are some organisations still finding it hard to recruit the right people? It has been my observation over the years that managers are not given the right tools to interview effectively.

Managers do not necessarily know how to interview. Have they checked their inherent bias at the door before they enter the interview room? Have they read the CV? Have they accepted the advice of HR? Recruitment/talent acquisition isn't an exact science, and even if we use all the tools noted above there is no guarantee you will have the desired outcome. Having the right people/person driving your process is key.

Ensure company values are built into the process and be clear about the type of individual you want before advertising. There are so many companies who get it wrong and end up wasting time in the process. What have your experiences been and what tips would you give an organisation?

Talent

Talent management, talent acquisition and talent pool: what do these terms really mean? The Chartered Institute of Personnel and Development (CIPD) defines talent management as: "the systematic attraction, identification, development, engagement, retention and deployment of those individuals who are of particular value to an organisation, either in view of their 'high potential' for the future or because they are fulfilling business/operation-critical roles".

The Recruiter.com notes:

"Talent Acquisition is the process of finding and acquiring skilled human labour for organisational needs and to meet any labour 'requirement'."

Finally, 'talent pool' is described by the *Cambridge Business English Dictionary* as "the suitable, skilled people who are available to be chosen to do a particular type of job".

Who are these exceptional people able to fall into these categories? It is you and me! Words like 'exceptional' and 'talent' are used to describe people who have shown a specific aptitude to a role that is deemed to be of high value to the organisation. Identifying the exceptionally talented allows HR and line managers to separate the good from the great when recruiting and developing those within the organisation who they believe can do more to develop their companies. Some are even given a fast-track opportunity to allow for speedy promotion.

What if we exchange the word 'talent' for 'employee management', 'employee acquisition', or even 'employee pool'? Not so 'sexy' I know, but this could give organisations an opportunity to look at everyone in the organisation. Maybe the phrase should be a 'talented organisation'. Whatever the phrase, if we see everyone as talented we can then start planning the strategy to make a talented organisation.

People Analysis - Job Analysis - Review - Training Needs Analysis - Develop - Promote - Support - Grow

I recently entered into email dialogue with a LinkedIn colleague who suggested that we need to look at the wider view of the world so we can see the hidden talents of individuals. The new surge in viewing diversity within an organisation as an important factor for growth goes some way to broadening the ideas of an organisation. Soon, more organisations can say they view their employees equally and give them the same opportunity. Well this is my hope.

Talent comes in various shapes and sizes. It isn't necessary to go for the obvious choices; let's look out for the little gems who can make an organisation great.

Redundancy: A Slippery Slope to Poor People Management

Redundancy is a challenging subject particularly as there are a lot of emotions that flow through this process from the individuals within the organisation that have to map out the redundancy to the person/s who are made redundant.

A fellow LinkedIn contact of mine wrote about the positive effect of being made redundant. It wasn't the process she was talking about, it was what happened to her afterwards. She took a leap of faith and her life changed positively. The redundancy experience however was not a happy one.

I also have a close friend who is a scientist who again experienced an organisational redundancy program which luckily did not affect her but many of her colleagues. The process was handled in such a way that I gasped every time she updated me on the situation. First, representatives of the executive team sent an email out to employees to inform them that they were being made redundant. They proceeded to thank everyone for their hard work thus far. A subsequent email said that a meeting with HR would be organised the following day to confirm which individuals had been affected. Meeting? Not quite. The affected employees were told to go into the HR office and were handed an envelope which had a pink slip and other information confirming the redundancy package.

What went wrong here? No consultation, no individual meetings with affected individuals, no support be it emotional or practical. In my opinion there was no considered approach to this. How would anyone know if they had selected individuals fairly? What was the selection process? As this happened close to Christmas you can imagine the upset their approach would have caused.

Unionised environments may stop these situations from arising as the unions act on behalf of their members. I do agree in principle with this statement however it really depends on the union. Some act defensively, others are more collaborative. Equally one would also have to comment, some organisations do not go into negotiations with unions openly or honestly.

Redundancy is a challenging process so why do some organisations make it harder to implement? How can we stop negative processes causing harm to individuals? Who takes care of those who suffer anxiety, stress, and depression because of a poorly thought-out procedure?

If we as HR professionals do not speak out against negative processes and procedures how can things change? Is the fear of being dismissed by employers so strong that we cannot be good advisors?

Accountability

I have had many discussions about the state of equality and diversity. One thing that is always constant is accountability. It is this word that stops good programmes becoming great programmes. This of course is not the only thing that needs to happen but it is fundamental.

Vance, Lowry, and Eggett (2015) note:

"Perceived need to justify one's behaviours to another party causes one to consider and feel accountable for the process by which decisions and judgments have been reached. In turn, this perceived need to account for a decision-making process and outcome increases the likelihood that one will think deeply and systematically about one's procedural behaviours."

So where is the accountability line in equality and diversity? There are schools of thought that HR should be accountable for the success of any undertaking in this area. CEOs are also seen to be a responsible party as they sanction the need for change. What about line managers? It is my belief that line managers can be the biggest blockage to any initiative around diversity. Negative behaviours are also reinforced by group managers' meetings, social events such as Friday drinking after work, and the need to report on the bottom line rather than the people.

I have had conversations with experts in equality and diversity where we have come to the same conclusion that if you do not address the line manager issue it is likely that the project will struggle because the blocker (line manager) doesn't see the importance of having a diverse workforce. Moreover they can easily bypass the request of the CEO or HR by implementing ineffective processes.

It is crucial to gain the line management's commitment when trying to institute diversity management policies since it is within the line manager's responsibility to implement HR policies effectively (Cox & Blake, 1991; Aries, 2004).

More work needs to be done to ensure that we do not overlook the need for the line managers to be fully engaged.

Accountability in my opinion and the opinion of others should be right across the business, CEO, directors, HR, line managers, and staff. A trail of accountability should be developed which will feed into data evidence to show the progression of the organisation. Any equality and diversity process should be embedded right through the organisation. It can then be monitored and challenges can be made for non-compliance.

I have often said equality and diversity is about human rights! We need to be accountable for our actions and ensure that those who try to drag the organisation down by their poor behaviours should be accountable for their actions too. Robust policies and procedures are a must as is alignment with the company values.

Clearly if you are not willing to change negative cultures, you cannot see the appropriateness of making sure there is a level playing field for everyone to achieve, and you do not want to give up your seat at the table to help someone else then there is a problem. Those who cherish such an environment come in many shapes, sizes, and colours. You may well be surprised that those who have protected characteristics and have been lucky enough to have a seat at the table sometimes build their empire and shake hands with those that prevent positive change.

It is indeed a challenging space to be in but those of us that want to make a difference will not accept all-white panels talking about diversity, production of data with no real action, segregation of characteristics to allow for just one to be favoured without supporting the rest. Collaboration is needed to increase the voice of equality and diversity. Do not be afraid to call out negative behaviours because if you do not, you become complicit.

Bibliography

Equality Act 2010
Public Disclosure Act 1998
Barbara S. Lawrence (1997:2), Perspective—The Black Box of Organisation Demography, Organisational Science
Google Web
Abraham Maslow (1943), A Theory of Human Motivation
Roger Kline (2014), Snowy White Peaks, Middlesex University Research Repository
Equality and Human Rights Commission 2016, Disability and Ethnicity Pay Gap
BBC News (January 2017) Report on Anna Wafula Strike, Paralympian
Leana Coopoosamy (2018), Gender Pay Gap. What about Ethnicity?
Macleans (Feb 2018), For Women of Colour, There's a Gap Within the Pay Gap
Joanna Wilde (March 2018), Racism at Work,
Afua Hirsch (August 2017), Guardian Newspaper, Ethnicity Pay Gap
ITN (July 2018), Ethnicity Pay Gap Reporting
Deloitte (December 2017), Ethnicity Pay Gap Reporting
BEIS Report (February 2017), Race in the Workplace
Rosa Monckton (March 2017), Spectator, Why People with Disabilities Should be Allowed to Work for Less
Professor Uta Frith, DBE, FBA, FMedSci, FRS (2015), Understanding Unconscious Bias, on behalf of The Royal Society
Stanford Encyclopaedia of Philosophy Study (2015), Implicit Bias
Psychology Today (2018), Bias
Oxford Dictionary (2018) Bias
recruiter.com, Talent Acquisition

Cambridge Business English Dictionary, Talent Pool
Anthony Vance, Paul Benjamin Lowry, and Dennis Eggett (2015). "A new approach to the problem of access policy violations: Increasing perceptions of accountability through the user interface."
(Cox & Blake, 1991; Aries, 2004), Management Commitment on Diversity

Printed in Great Britain
by Amazon